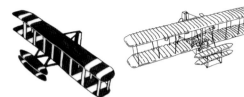

Stories of GREAT PEOPLE

The Wright Brothers' glider

Gerry Bailey and Karen Foster
Illustrated by Leighton Noyes
and Karen Radford

Crabtree Publishing Company
www.crabtreebooks.com

Mr. RUMMAGE has a stall piled high with interesting objects—and he has a great story to tell about each and every one of his treasures.

DIGBY PLATT is an antique collector. Every Saturday he picks up a bargain at Mr. Rummage's antique stall and loves listening to the story behind his new 'find'.

HANNAH PLATT is Digby's argumentative, older sister—and she doesn't believe a word that Mr. Rummage says!

Mr. POLLOCK's toy stall is filled with string puppets, rocking horses, model planes, wooden animals—and he makes them all himself!

Crabtree Publishing Company
www.crabtreebooks.com

Other books in the series

Cleopatra's coin

Columbus's chart

Martin Luther King, Jr.'s microphone

Leonardo's palette

Armstrong's moon rock

Shakespeare's quill

Marco Polo's silk purse

Mother Teresa's alms bowl

Sitting Bull's tomahawk

Credits

cover: NASA
Corbis: 11 center left
Library of Congress: 9 top, 11 top right, 19 bottom left, 19 top right, 24 bottom, 28 top, 31 bottom right, 32 center
Lilienthal Museum: 23 top
Mary Evans Picture Library: 9 bottom, 13 top left
NASA: 27 top, 27 bottom, 28 bottom, 31 bottom left
Picturepoint/Topfoto: 12 center right
Science Museum/Science & Society Picture Library: 20 top
Science Photo Library: 9 center left, 9 center right
Tekniska Museet, Sweden: 14 bottom left
UPP/Topfoto: 20 bottom
US Air Force: 24 top

Picture research: Diana Morris info@picture-research.co.uk

Library and Archives Canada Cataloguing in Publication

Bailey, Gerry
        The Wright Brothers' glider / Gerry Bailey and Karen Foster ; illustrated by Leighton Noyes and Karen Radford.

(Stories of great people)
Includes index.
ISBN 978-0-7787-3693-6 (bound).--ISBN 978-0-7787-3715-5 (pbk.)

        1. Wright, Orville, 1871-1948--Juvenile fiction. 2. Wright, Wilbur, 1867-1912--Juvenile fiction. 3. Aeronautics--United States--Biography--Juvenile fiction. 4. Inventors--United States--Biography--Juvenile fiction. I. Foster, Karen, 1959- II. Noyes, Leighton III. Radford, Karen IV. Title. V. Series.

PZ7.B15Wr 2008   j823'.92   C2007-907629-7

Library of Congress Cataloging-in-Publication Data

Bailey, Gerry.
  The Wright brothers' glider / Gerry Bailey and Karen Foster ; illustrated by Leighton Noyes and Karen Radford.
        p. cm. -- (Stories of great people)
  Includes index.
  ISBN-13: 978-0-7787-3693-6 (rlb)
  ISBN-10: 0-7787-3693-8 (rlb)
  ISBN-13: 978-0-7787-3715-5 (pb)
  ISBN-10: 0-7787-3715-2 (pb)
  1. Wright, Orville, 1871-1948--Juvenile literature. 2. Wright, Wilbur, 1867-1912--Juvenile literature. 3. Aeronautics--United States--Biography--Juvenile literature. 4. Inventors--United States--Biography--Juvenile literature. I. Foster, Karen, 1959- II. Noyes, Leighton, ill. III. Radford, Karen, ill. IV. Title.
  TL540.W7B35 2008
  629.130092'2--dc22
  [B]
                                2007051265

Crabtree Publishing Company

www.crabtreebooks.com   1-800-387-7650

Published in Canada
Crabtree Publishing
616 Welland Ave.
St. Catharines, Ontario
L2M 5V6

Published in the United States
Crabtree Publishing
PMB16A
350 Fifth Ave., Suite 3308
New York, NY 10118

Published by CRABTREE PUBLISHING COMPANY
Copyright © **2008** Diverta Ltd.

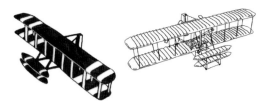

The Wright Brothers' Glider

Table of Contents

"Every Saturday morning, Knicknack Market comes to life. The street vendors are there almost before the sun is up. And by the time you and I are out of bed, the stalls are built, the boxes are opened, and all the goods are carefully laid out on display.

Objects are piled high. Some are laid out on velvet: precious necklaces and jeweled swords. Others stand upright at the back: large, framed pictures of very important people, lamps made from tasseled satin, and old-fashioned cash registers—the kind that jingle when the drawers are opened.

And then there are things that stay in their boxes all day, waiting for the right customer to come along: war medals laid out in straight lines, or utensils in polished silver for all those special occasions.

But Mr. Rummage's stall is different. Rummage of Knicknack Market has a stall piled high with a disorderly jumble of things that no one could ever want. Who'd want to buy a stuffed mouse? Or a broken umbrella? Or a pair of false teeth? Well, Mr. Rummage has them all!

"Digby Platt—ten-year-old collector of antiques—was on his way to see his friend Mr. Rummage of Knicknack Market. It was Saturday and, as usual, Digby's weekly allowance was burning a hole in his pocket. Digby wasn't going to spend it on any old thing. It had to be something rare and interesting for his collection, something from Mr. Rummage's incredible stall.

Hannah, his older sister, had come along, too. She had secret doubts about the value of Mr. Rummage's objects and felt, for some big-sisterly reason, that she had to stop her little brother from buying junk.

"Hi Mr. Rummage," shouted Digby as soon as he saw his friend's stall. "Are you there?"

"You're here bright and early," said a voice as they passed by the toy shop. "I've been up all night fixing this. Here, give me a hand."

"Hi Mr. Pollock," said Hannah to the toy maker. "What are you fixing?"

"Looks like a model plane to me— a **glider**," said Mr. Rummage, who'd just strolled across from his stall on the opposite sidewalk.

"It is a glider, Mr. Rummage. It's a model made by the great Wright brothers, Wilbur and Orville."

"Wow!" exclaimed Hannah, who loved the idea of flying. "Is it really one of their planes?"

"Of course," said Mr. Pollock, beaming with pride. "It's the real thing."

THE WRIGHT BROTHERS

On April 16, 1867, Milton and Susan Wright welcomed a third child into their home near Millville, Indiana. The newest member of the family, whom they called Wilbur, had two elder brothers—Reuchlin and Lorin. Little did Susan know that she had given birth to the first half of one of the world's most famous inventive partnerships. The other half of the duo, Orville, was born four years later on August 19, 1871, in the family's newly built home in Dayton, Ohio. Orville's sister, Katharine, was born in the same house on Orville's third birthday.

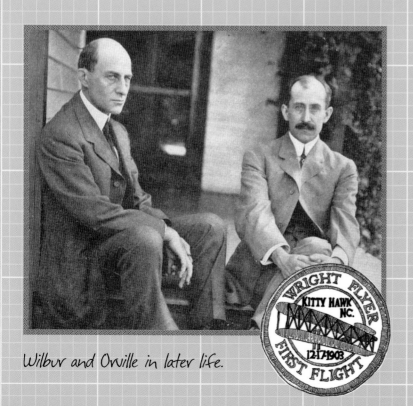

Wilbur and Orville with their father, Milton, above.

KINGS OF THE AIR

Although the Wright brothers didn't build the first aircraft, they did build the first one that could be controlled over a distance. This was very important because it meant men could finally fly in the air–just like birds. The Wrights became famous for the innovative flying machines they pioneered.

Wilbur and Orville in later life.

Let's find out more...

"What strange names!" exclaimed Hannah.

"They were given unusual first names because their parents decided not to give them middle names," Mr. Pollock explained. "In fact, both were named after clergymen whom their father, Milton, admired. They were known as "Will" and "Orv" to their friends, but they used to call each other "Ullam" and "Bubs"—for no good reason that I know of. Who knows how the minds of great inventors work!"

"I still think they're weird names," said Hannah.

"Anyway," interrupted Mr. Rummage, "their mother didn't have an unusual name. She was called something very simple—Susan. She was a carriage maker's daughter and a great mechanic in her own right. In fact, she was the one who taught the boys to make things. Her husband, Milton, was not a very handy man."

"So the boys inherited all their mechanical ability from their mother," said Hannah, looking at her brother triumphantly.

"Yes, they did," agreed Mr. Rummage and Mr. Pollock together.

A PREACHER ON THE MOVE

Milton Wright was a church minister, a teacher, and a missionary. He traveled a lot before marrying Susan and having seven children. In fact, the family moved twelve times before finally settling in Dayton, Ohio. Milton was chosen to edit the church newspaper, the *Religious Telescope*. He did well at this and was made a bishop of the church. The neighbors in Dayton knew his children simply as "the bishop's kids."

The family home at 7 Hawthorn Street in Dayton.

A LARGE LIBRARY

The boys used their father's huge library and spent many hours with their heads in a book. Their love of adventure stories fed their imaginations and probably encouraged them to explore new ideas. The two became fascinated by stories of flight. There was one tale about the Greek hero, Daedalus, who flew too close to the sun and had his wings scorched. Then there was King Kaj Kaoos of Persia, who attached eagles to his throne so he could fly around his kingdom. Not to mention the Birdman of Ulm, a German tailor who made himself a pair of wings and threw himself into the wind from the spire of the city's cathedral, falling to his death.

Susan Wright, mother of Orville and Wilbur.

CLOSE-KNIT

Orville and Wilbur were close to each other all their lives. Wilbur wrote in his diary that they lived together, played together, worked together, and even thought together. Everything they achieved was the result of conversations they'd had or things they'd done together..

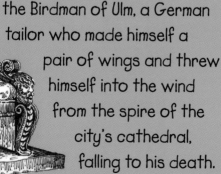
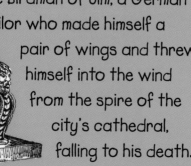

"One day, Milton returned from his travels with a toy helicopter for the boys. It became their favorite. It probably sparked their early interest in flight and flying machines."

"But helicopters didn't exist back then, Mr. Pollock," said Hannah, "so how could Milton have found one?"

"Yes, well it didn't look anything like the helicopters we know today. It was just a toy," said Mr. Pollock, pulling one out of his pocket.

"I see," said Hannah, examining it closely. "It does look a little strange…"

"Stupid!" said Digby. "Of course it's not real. The plane hadn't been invented yet!"

"Remember Leonardo da Vinci?" said Hannah. "He invented a helicopter, so there!"

"You're right, young lady," interrupted Mr. Rummage. "But let's stick to the Wrights!"

A WONDERFUL TOY

The helicopter-like toy that Milton brought home for his boys was based on an invention by the French **aeronautical** pioneer, Alphonse Penaud. It was made of paper, bamboo, and cork, with a rubber band that could be wound up to "twirl" its blades. It was no bigger than an adult's hand. Apparently Wilbur and Orville played with it so much that it finally broke, so they had to build one of their own.

Leonardo's design for an aerial screw.

LEONARDO'S AERIAL SCREW

Leonardo da Vinci, the great Italian inventor and genius, made the first real studies of flight in the 1480s. He studied birds and made over 100 drawings illustrating his ideas. His aerial screw was never built, although the modern day helicopter is based on his idea.

A painting of the prophet Elijah, caught in a whirlwind.

Elijah's chariot of fire

MYTHS ABOUT FLIGHT

There are many myths about winged men and other curious creatures. In Celtic myths, for example, the Sluagh were a group of flying evil spirits that haunted the living and hunted the souls of sinners. According to a Chinese legend, Yu-Ren was an immortal man covered in feathers, which helped him to fly. Smaj, a winged man who spits fire, is the guardian of Serbia. Kanae, in Polynesian mythology, was a semi spirit with the power to transform himself into a flying fish. Sheikh Ali was a Malaysian king who ruled three kingdoms: the kingdom of flying horses, the kingdom of flying lions, and the kingdom of flying elephants. Then there was Mercury, the Roman messenger of the gods. He usually wore sandals with wings on them and a winged helmet.

FLIGHTS OF IMAGINATION

Milton encouraged the boys to make things, even though he was not good at it himself. But it was through listening to their father's sermons in church every Sunday that the boys heard the story of the Hebrew prophet Elijah—one of many stories in the Bible about flight. In the story, Elijah was picked up by a chariot and horses of fire and went up to heaven in a whirlwind. This story, as well as many others, captured the boys' imaginations and stimulated their interest in mechanical tools and games.

THE HISTORY OF FLIGHT

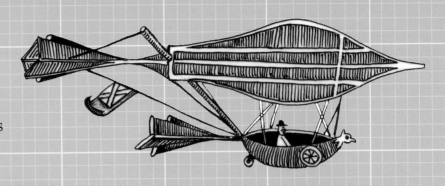

Wilbur and Orville studied the successes and failures of early flying machines.

MONTGOLFIERS' BALLOON

The French brothers Joseph and Etienne Montgolfier invented the first hot air balloon. They used the smoke from a fire to blow hot air into a silk bag attached to a basket. The hot air then rose and allowed the balloon to be lighter than air. In 1783, they sent up their first passengers—a sheep, rooster, and a duck! The flight was successful.

The first flight of the Mongolfiers' balloon.

GEORGE CAYLEY'S GLIDER

The English engineer George Cayley designed a helicopter with rotating propellers in 1796. Eight years later, he built a model monoplane glider, which looked very modern for the times. The plane had a movable cross-tail, and a kite-shaped wing. Over the years, he tried a lot of wing shapes and he discovered that wings with a curved surface would lift a plane higher than wings with a flat surface could. He built a large gliding machine and tested it, first with a 10-year-old boy and then with his coach driver aboard!

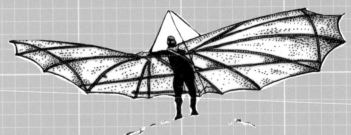

LILIENTHAL'S HANG GLIDER

In the 1880s, the German engineer Otto Lilienthal was the first person to design a hang glider that could fly a person over long distances. He crashed many times during his 2,500 trial runs. In the end, he fell to his death when he lost control of his glider in a sudden gust of strong wind. However, his courage and his research inspired the Wrights to come up with ideas of their own.

"Did the Wright boys go to school?" asked Digby. "Or did they just look at books in the library all day?"

"Wilbur went to school when he was eight," said Mr. Rummage. "He learned to ice-skate well, do gymnastics, and fly kites. His father wrote that he was quick to learn, concentrated well, and also had a great memory."

"It sounds as if he was a whiz kid," said Hannah.

"Well, his father had big plans for him. But one day, while Wilbur was skating, a hockey stick flew out of someone's hand and struck Wilbur in the mouth. Three weeks later, the doctor said he had a weak heart and should take it easy. So Wilbur left school and began studying at home."

"He must have been lonely," said Digby.

"Maybe. But he also had to look after his mother, who was very ill," Mr. Rummage went on.

"Orville wasn't quite so bright. He also got into trouble and had to sit at the front of the class so his teacher could keep an eye on him. When he left school at seventeen, he opened his own print shop. Later, he started up a newspaper."

"Children are always lucky if they have people around who encourage them to learn and use their imaginations." added Mr. Pollock. "I was lucky like that and it meant I could pursue my interest in toys— as you see."

"Those old balloons and gliders were really cool," said Digby, full of enthusiasm. "I'd like to see more of them."

"All right, Digby," said Mr. Pollock. "I've got models of all kinds of flying machines at my stall. Come with me and I'll show them to you. Will you join us, Mr. Rummage?"

"Of course," said Mr. Rummage, following the children to Mr. Pollock's toy stall.

"That's beautiful. What is it?" asked Hannah, pointing at a colorful toy, hanging from the roof of the stall.

"That's Jacques Charles's hydrogen balloon," said Mr. Pollock. "Half the population of Paris watched it go up!"

"I wish I'd been there," said Digby. "It looks like more fun than taking off in an airplane."

"Yes. But I think you'd have found that touching down while still in one piece was more of a problem!" laughed Mr. Rummage.

"And over here's a hang glider much like the ones Otto Lilienthal experimented with," Mr. Pollock went on, dangling a model with wide, canvas wings. "He'd be surprised to know how many people hang glide as a hobby today."

"Well, I like this one," said Mr. Rummage, holding a melon-shaped balloon.

"Ah yes, an airship, or blimp, as they used to call them. One of those could carry about 10 passengers, you know."

"What's this Mr. Pollock? It looks like a paper airplane," said Digby.

"Doesn't look like much of an invention to me," grumbled Hannah. "I could make one of those myself!"

"Actually, it's a model of George Cayley's glider," said Mr. Pollock. "He was the engineer who put a boy of ten into the cockpit and sent him up in a test flight—remember?"

"It must have been really dangerous up there when no one really knew how to build a plane," said Hannah.

"Oh yes, you had to be very brave," agreed Mr. Pollock, "but this was an exciting time for flight, and the Wright brothers were excited—although at one point it seemed they might have done something completely different…"

"You mean they had a day job?" asked Hannah.

"Sort of," laughed Mr. Rummage. "In fact, the first time the boys labeled themselves 'The Wright Brothers' was when Wilbur joined Orville at his printing company. But that didn't stop them from inventing many different machines."

"That's right," continued Mr. Pollock, "they even built their own printing press."

"Out of an old kitchen sink, I suppose," said Hannah.

"No, from a broken tombstone and parts of a baby carriage." said Mr. Pollock, "which was much more exciting."

"What did they print on their press?" asked Digby.

"They produced a four-page weekly called the *West Side News*, Mr. Rummage replied. "And they used the money they made to finance their research on flight. But they did something else first."

"Yes, they decided to open a bicycle repair shop," said Mr. Pollock. "Cycling was becoming a popular hobby in those days, and they liked fooling around with bike parts in their backyard."

"It sounds as though they couldn't make up their minds what they wanted to do," said Hannah.

"I think they just enjoyed making things work," said Mr. Pollock. "Eventually they made their own bicycles, which they named the Nan Cleeve and the St. Clair. Great names, don't you think?"

SELF-TAUGHT MECHANICAL ENGINEERS

Through their work at the printing press and the bicycle repair shop, the Wright brothers quickly became self-taught **mechanical engineers**. But they liked a challenge, so once they'd mastered one task, they'd move on to the next. They loved solving problems. And how to fly was the problem they most wanted to solve.

The Wright's safety bike.

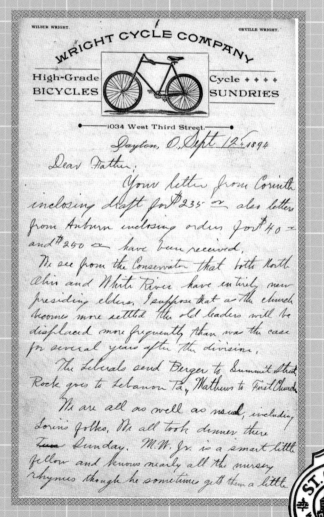

A letter from Wilbur to his father.

THE SAFETY BICYCLE

When the safety bicycle—a bike with two wheels of equal size—was invented, America went wild for cycling. Wilbur and Orville bought one each and joined a cycling club. By now they had built up a reputation as mechanics, so friends soon began asking them to repair their bicycles. This allowed them to start up their bike repair business. It wasn't long before the brothers decided they could do a better job of building a bike than the manufacturers whose bikes they repaired. So they did, building handmade bicycles to order, and making a good living out of it.

BIKES AND PLANES

In the 19th century, people thought that the problems that held back human flight were similar to the problems faced by learner cyclists. Trying to master a bike was so tricky that it seemed to the average person to be just as impossible as flying.

EARLY FLYING MACHINES

LILIENTHAL'S BIRD BOOK

Otto Lilienthal wrote about the flight of birds, especially storks, and drew diagrams describing the shape of their wings and how it affects the way the air moves around them. His experiments with gliders helped to prove that heavier-than-air flight was possible without flapping wings. The Wright brothers were fascinated by *Flight of Birds*, and experimented with some of the ideas inside it.

CHANUTE'S BOOK ON FLYING MACHINES

The American engineer, Octave Chanute, published his book *Progress in Flying Machines* in 1894. It was the first ever collection of technical know-how from the world's aviation pioneers. It was a bestseller, and the Wrights used it as a basis for their own experiments. Chanute also made bi-wing and tri-wing gliders. He took them to the shore of Lake Michigan, where he used young flying enthusiasts like himself to test them.

The Chanute-Herring glider was nicknamed the "double-decker" by the Wright brothers because it had two wing surfaces.

Langley's plane was launched by catapult from the top of a houseboat.

SAMUEL LANGLEY'S AERODROME

The American inventor Samuel Langley managed to successfully fly an unmanned, steam-powered model aircraft. Later, he produced an engine-powered craft called the Aerodrome. It had wire-braced **tandem** wings, one behind the other, and was launched into the air by a catapult. But the piloted craft had no landing gear, so in order to avoid fatal accidents, Langley tested it over the Potomac River. He gave up on his project when the Aerodrome fell into the river "like a handful of wet cement" in 1903.

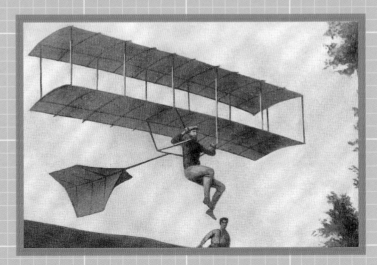

"**S**o when, exactly, did the Wright brothers actually start to make flying machines?" asked Digby impatiently.

"Well, it's a long story" said Mr. Pollock. "If my memory's right, it was in 1896 that Orville became sick with Typhoid fever. It was a serious illness. But Wilbur took care of his brother and read him stories about the dramatic flights of German glider pilot Otto Lilienthal to cheer him up."

"But I thought the Wright brothers were the first ones to invent flying," said Digby, looking disappointed.

"Birds were the first to do that," said Mr. Pollock. "Then there were the hot air balloons, of course. And, you're right. Lilienthal just glided. He couldn't actually power his gliders like birds power their wings. He could control a few things, but he had no power. So powered flight—the kind that really mattered—still hadn't been invented."

"Ah, that's good," smiled Digby with relief. "I wanted the Wrights to be first."

"Wilbur became so fascinated with the idea of flight," Mr. Pollock went on, "that he wrote to the Smithsonian Institute in New York. The Smithsonian is the world's largest science museum and Wilbur knew he would find what he wanted there. He asked for every piece of aeronautical information they had."

"And in just a few months," added Mr. Rummage, "he had read everything there was to know about flying."

"Wilbur and Orville spent a lot of time reading about birds and watching them fly," said Mr. Pollock.

"Just like my birdbrained brother," said Hannah.

"Really, do you like ornithology young man?' said Mr. Pollock asked Digby.

"What's orni…ornith…whatever?"

"It's the study of ornithopters, silly," said Hannah.

"Actually, it's the study of birds," said Mr. Rummage, "their wing shapes, and how they move through the air."

"Yes," agreed Mr. Pollock, "and the brothers soon learned that the best way to turn a flying machine in the air was to bank, or lean the thing into the turn, just like a bird does."

"Like this?" said Digby as he ran around with his arms spread, screaming airplane noises, leaning first the one way and then another.

"Exactly, Digby!" cried the toy maker with a chuckle. Hannah just put her fingers in her ears.

FLY LIKE A BIRD

BALANCING ACT

The Wright brothers knew that flying was all about balance. If a flying machine tilted to one side in the wind, it usually crashed because the machine couldn't recover or balance again. By watching how birds balance their bodies in the air, the brothers hoped to solve the problem.

WINDMILL WINGS

Wilbur worked out that birds adjust the tips of their wings as they fly, to create an upturned angle on one side and a turned down angle on the other side. The wings work like a kind of windmill to turn the bird in the air. When it comes out of a turn, the bird reverses the angles of both wing tips to regain its balance.

Lilienthal was nicknamed the "Birdman" because of the wings he flew with.

BIRDMAN DISASTER

Lilienthal fell to his death when the wind upset the balance of his glider. This and other disasters made the Wrights even more determined to find the answer. Eventually, they concluded that reliable pilot control, not built-in stability, was the key to successful, safe flight.

BIPLANE BOX

One day, Wilbur picked up an old, cardboard box. Holding the rectangular box in his hands, he squeezed the corners diagonal to each other. He noticed that when one end turned up, the other automatically turned down. The box had twisted. He then imagined the sides of the box as the wings of a **biplane**. Soon he realized that, with a set of cables, he could twist, or warp, the wings and they'd work in the same way as a bird's wings.

GOOD NEWS

Wilbur was so excited by what he had achieved, he couldn't wait to tell Orville, who was camping with friends. So he rode his bike out to the campsite to tell him the good news. Immediately, the brothers began planning a glider that would use the new twisting controls.

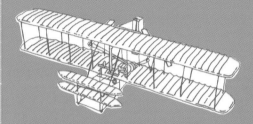

The Wright brothers drew diagrams to work out the answers to technical problems. This blueprint is of their 1903 Flyer.

WIND TUNNEL

The Wrights built a **wind tunnel** and tested over 200 different wing shapes in it to see which one worked best.

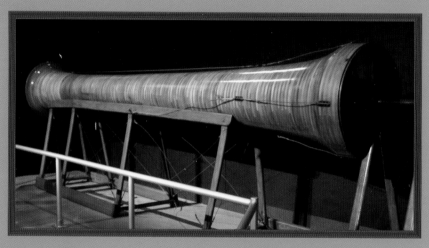

the Wrights' wind tunnel

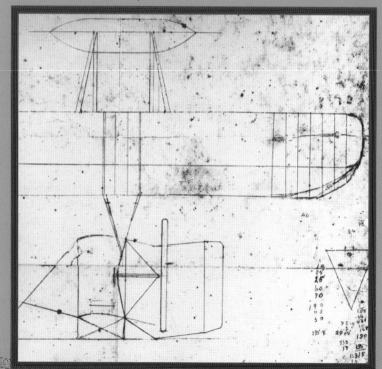

AN ELEGANT SOLUTION

Wilbur's "warped wing" answer to the flight control problem was just one of many discoveries the Wright brothers made. Today, engineers call their control solution the "elegant solution." At last, Wilbur had solved a problem that had troubled many aeronautical engineers.

"Awesome" said Digby with a grin. "So now that the Wrights could control the wings of a plane, maybe they could fly."

"They were getting there," said Mr. Pollock. "Wilbur and Orville started their experiments in 1896 with kites and gliders."

"I bet Wilbur tried to build a new model plane right away," said Hannah.

"Yes, he did," said Mr. Pollock. "In a matter of days, he built a box kite that looked a little like a biplane with controls that would roll it. He also included a movable tail so they could make it go up or down."

"That's called the pitch," said Digby. "I learned that at school."

"Correct," continued Mr. Pollock. "The control lines ran between the four corners of the kite and were attached to two sticks. Wilbur held one in each hand. When he turned the sticks in opposite directions, the wings would twist and make the kite roll left or right. When the sticks were turned in the same direction, he could move the tail up or down, making the kite rise or fall."

"But did it work?" asked Hannah.

"Wilbur took it out on a windy fall day," said Mr. Rummage, "and it worked perfectly. At last, he could control the flight of his model!"

"The the boys started by making gliders," said Mr. Pollock. "They tested them at a place called Kitty Hawk because of the good flying conditions there, but also because it was a lonely spot, far from curious eyes."

"Why did that worry them?" asked Hannah.

"Well, there was a race on to see who'd be the first to invent a powered airplane that could be controlled. Orville and Wilbur didn't want anyone to steal their ideas or beat them to the finishing line."

"Their first gliders had two wings, what we now call biplanes," added Mr. Rummage.

"Unfortunately, though, they didn't lift very far off the ground and were difficult to control," said Mr. Pollock. "So they built a wind tunnel."

"Like the ones they use in NASCAR racing?" asked Digby.

"Not quite as complicated," said Mr. Rummage, "but good enough to experiment with hundreds of wing shapes. Their third glider was the first ever fully controllable aircraft. It had roll, yaw, and pitch controls."

"A marvel of engineering," said Mr. Pollock, "It flew a record 623 feet (190 m)!"

"Amazing!" said Hannah.

The very first flight took place at Kitty Hawk.

KITTY HAWK

Once he'd built his glider, Wilbur needed a place to fly it. He chose Kitty Hawk in North Carolina because the winds there were often high—perfect for launching a glider. There was also soft sand underfoot, which would cushion the blow of a rough landing.

The Congressional medal was awarded for the the Wrights' first flight.

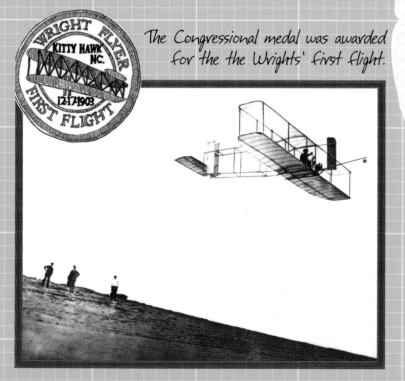

LYING-FLATOUT

The pilot of the Wrights' first gliders lay flat, headfirst on the lower-wing. He did this to reduce **aerodynamic** drag, or to make it more streamlined. When the glider came in to land, the pilot was supposed to hang on to the supports and pull himself upright through a hole in the wing so he could land on his feet. But the brothers found that they could stay lying down without any real danger. That's how they made all their flights for the first five years.

UN-PILOTED

In the beginning, no one piloted the gliders. Instead, the brothers used sandbags and chains as ballast, or weight, on the machines. They did one test with the glider suspended from a small homemade tower. Once, they used a local boy as ballast, apparently he didn't count as a human pilot!

27

PERFECTING THE FLYING MACHINE

When Orville and Wilbur returned from their historic flight at Kitty Hawk, they knew they still had a lot to do to perfect their machine. They set up a test flight base at Huffman Prairie, a large field northeast of Dayton. It became the world's first test flight facility. They made many flights, fine-tuning the controls, engine, propellers, and other parts of the aircraft.

Orville flying over Huffman Prairie
November 16, 1904

FIRST CIRCULAR FLIGHT

The first flights could only be made in a straight line and took less than a minute before the pilot had to land. Then, on September 20, 1904, Wilbur flew in a complete circle that took about a minute and a half. It was the first circular flight in history. By the end of 1905, the aircraft could be flown in figure eights and remain in the air for over half an hour.

PRACTICAL PLANE

The 1905 aircraft, called the Wright Flyer, was good enough to be sold to someone else. It was the first practical aircraft and in 1906, the brothers received a **patent** for the Wright flying machine. Now, Wilbur and Orville had to look for people to buy their wonderful invention.

the Wright Flyer outside its **hangar** at the test flight base

28

"Now all they needed was power," said Digby.

"So why didn't they flap their arms?" asked Hannah, "or tie a flock of pigeons to the wings?"

"Great ideas, Hannah," said Mr. Pollock, "but I don't think they'd work, do you?" Anyway, a mechanic helped them to build a small, light engine and a propeller—just the things to power their plane. Then they shipped the parts down to Kitty Hawk, where it was put together."

"But when they got there they found they had competition!" said Mr. Rummage. "A man called Sam Langley had built his own powered aircraft!"

"Oh no," cried Digby. "What did they do?"

"Well, luckily for the Wrights, Langley's effort was a miserable failure. He gave up and left the Wrights to it."

"So now they could really takeoff," said Hannah enthusiastically.

"That's right," said Mr. Pollock. "On December 14, 1903, Wilbur won a coin toss that allowed him to make the first attempt to fly the machine. But he stalled on takeoff and caused some damage to the plane. It was repaired by December 17, and at 10:35 a.m. on a cold, windy morning, Orville made the first heavier-than-air, machine-powered flight ever!"

"Yeah!" cried the kids as they clapped and jumped up and down.

"The flight wasn't long," added Mr. Rummage, "just 120 feet (36.6 m) in 12 seconds. But Orville had finally done what people had dreamed of doing for centuries."

29

"Now, of course, everyone wanted to jump on the flying machine bandwagon," said Mr. Pollock. "Greedy people realized that inventing could make them very rich."

"I bet everyone wanted to build a plane," said Hannah.

"Yes, but no one could match the Wright brothers' flying machines," said Mr. Rummage.

"The problem was," said Mr. Pollock, "the brothers wasted a lot of time fighting for patents and sorting out legal problems."

"What's a patent?" asked Digby.

"A patent is a certificate all inventors need to prove they own their ideas, so that no one else can use them," explained Mr. Pollock.

"Unfortunately, the brothers had shared their ideas with Glenn Curtiss of the Aerial Experiment Association," added Mr. Rummage. "And very soon, Curtiss started building planes of his own. He even won awards with them. The brothers were furious, of course. In fact, they took him to court for trying to copy their designs."

FLYING DEMOS

The Wrights soon realized that their planes might be useful to the military. But if they wanted to sell their designs to the U.S. Army, they knew they had to give a lot of flying demonstrations. So, while Orville gave exhibitions in the United States, Wilbur went to France, where he hoped to sell aircraft. He made record-breaking flights near Le Mans in 1908 and impressed the crowds. The result was an agreement with the French government to construct flying machines in their country.

The Wright brothers' patent certificate proved that their ideas belonged to them.

DISASTER!

Meanwhile, Orville stayed in the United States to give demonstrations and try to win over the army. He was successful, but it nearly cost him his life. On a flight at Fort Meyer, Orville lost a propeller and the plane crashed. Lt. Thomas Selfridge, his passenger, died in the accident. Luckily, Orville only broke a leg.

This page of the Wright brothers' scrapbook shows Wilbur flying around the Statue of Liberty in New York Harbor.

A ROUNDTRIP

Once Orville recovered, he and Wilbur took a new military plane to Fort Meyer. They used it to successfully complete the military trials. A few months later, Wilbur put on a spectacular air show in New York Harbor. He flew from Grosvenor Island to the Statue of Liberty and Grant's Tomb. The public were amazed and the Wright brothers became huge celebrities.

EXHIBITION PILOTS

The Wrights hired teams of pilots to fly in their air shows. They knew that this was how a lot of money could be made. But the more the public got used to aircraft, the riskier the stunts they demanded from the pilots.

ticket to a Wright brothers' air show.

THE WRIGHT TEAM

The opening show was held at the Indianapolis Motor Speedway on June 13, 1910. The shows went on for just over a year. There were a number of accidents. One plane crashed with the mayor of Virginia aboard. When the program ended in November, 1911, five of the Wright's nine pilots had died in crashes.

FASTER, HIGHER, LOWER

Pilots had to fly faster, lower, and perform more death-defying tricks in order to satisfy their audiences. But the more reckless they became, the more likely they were to hurt themselves. The Wrights became more and more anxious about this, and Wilbur's health began to suffer.

"The Wright brothers really started something big, didn't they, Mr. Pollock. No wonder they were celebrities."

"They did, Digby," agreed Mr. Pollock. "In fact, they completely changed the way people thought about transport. All of a sudden they could travel in a straight line—'as the crow flies.'"

"Ha ha, very funny," giggled Hannah. "Although Wilbur does look a little like a crow, doesn't he?"

"I guess," said Mr. Pollock, "but a famous crow. Anyway, when he and Orville returned to Dayton, they were given a two-day gala celebration and awarded a Congressional Gold Medal by the government."

"Wow," said Digby, "that's really cool."
"Well, they'd created something that captured everyone's imagination," Mr. Rummage went on. "Pilots became heroes by doing stunts and taking part in air shows. Businesses understood that planes could become a popular means of transportation in the future. The army saw aircraft's military potential. Even artists were attracted by the beauty of the machines and their movement in the air."

"Did their father, Milton ever fly?" asked Digby.

"He did. On May 25, 1910, at Huffman Prairie, Orville made two special flights. First, he took his 82-year-old father on his one and only flight. They flew to 350 feet (107 m) while his father called out "Higher, Orville, higher!" Then Orville made a six-minute flight with his brother as a passenger. This was special because they'd always promised their dad they'd never fly together, just in case their plane crashed. One brother had to stay alive to carry out experiments, you see."

"Of course," said Hannah.

"What a shame," exclaimed Digby, "but I suppose flying was still risky back then."

"The whole thing would have been stopped after just one accident these days," agreed Mr. Rummage. "Anyway, as business problems piled up, the Wrights became worn out. And they weren't even producing the best aircraft anymore."

"Too busy worrying to invent," said Mr. Pollock. "Then in 1912, Wilbur got Typhoid fever and died."

"Oh no," said Hannah, "poor Orville. What did he do?"

"Sadly, Orville's heart wasn't in the aviation business after his brother's death," said Mr. Rummage. "So he sold the company and went back to inventing."

"Good for him," said Hannah.

"What else did he invent?" asked Digby.

"Well, he built a small lab back in Dayton and worked on anything that interested him. He made children's toys, a toaster, and even a guided missile. But he still did some airplane work."

"I'm glad he did," said Digby, picking up the model glider and giving Mr. Pollock a coin. "Come on, Wilbur," he said to his sister, "I've got a really cool idea for a plane with invisible wings."

"Oh no…" groaned Hannah.

SUCCESS STORY

In 1916, when Orville sold his interests in the Wright Company, he used his fame to get onto the board of the National Advisory Committee for Aeronautics, or NACA, which later became NASA. He also helped with the Guggenheim fund that promoted aeronautics. He was a member of the U.S. Naval Consulting Board and, with what time he had left, he helped young aspiring inventors.

MEMORABILIA

Orville Wright died on January 30, 1948. He and his brother left behind 11 huge scrapbooks bulging with newspaper clippings as well as cartoons, guest badges, posters, telegrams, and stamps. They also left many diaries, notebooks, and papers that told of their research and invention of the first powered, controllable, heavier-than-air machine.

THE CASE FOR AND AGAINST

WERE THEY THE FIRST?

Many people believe that the Wright brothers invented the first airplane. But not everyone is convinced. The fact that the brothers had to keep their inventions secret while patents were being prepared, made some people suspicious about their motives.

WAS THEIR FLIGHT REALLY FLYING?

Then there are people who question whether the Wright brothers' early flights actually flew high enough to be considered off the ground. Others point out that the Wrights' early flights were made into the wind, which helped lift the craft. However, taking off into the wind soon became standard practice in aviation, as it was clearly the safest way.

COULD THEIR CONSTRUCTION FLY?

Another argument against the Wrights is that reconstructions of their original Flyer don't fly. However, as no one knows the exact details of the Wrights' design and construction, it's impossible to duplicate the plane and the flight.

WAS IT A REAL TAKEOFF?

After Kitty Hawk, the Wrights constructed a kind of catapult to help their aircraft takeoff faster. Wheels didn't help the Flyer takeoff in the place where it was being tested, so the brothers used rails and then the catapult to help. Some argue that if a plane can't takeoff under its own power, it doesn't count as a real plane. But Flyer II did takeoff without a catapult and made many flights in 1904.

The Wrights invented reliable controls and made true flight—with turns, circles, and figure eights—possible sooner.

WAS IT THE FIRST TO ACTUALLY FLY?

A few heavier-than-air flying machines probably did become airborne before the Wrights' machines. But these lacked controls. The Wright Flyer was the first flying machine that combined new features such as wings, three-axis control, a power source, and a takeoff system. All of these features were included in aircraft that came later.

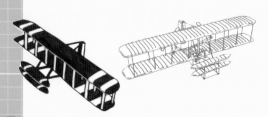

GLOSSARY

aerodynamic Describing vehicles with smooth sides and rounded edges so wind flows over them without slowing them down

aeronautical Relating to the design and construction of aircraft

biplane An airplane having two pairs of wings fixed at different levels, especially one above and one below the main body of the aircraft

glider A light engineless aircraft designed to glide after being towed into the air or launched from a catapult

hangar A shelter especially for housing or repairing aircraft

mechanical engineer A person who is specially trained to design machines and tools

patent A grant made by a government that gives the creator of an invention the right to be the only one to make, use, and sell that invention for a set period of time

tandem An arrangement of two or more persons or objects placed one behind the other

wind tunnel A tube-shaped chamber that air is forced through at controlled velocities in order to study how air flows around models or other objects

INDEX

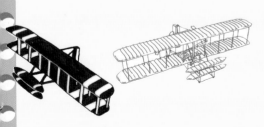

Other characters in the Stories of Great People series.

SAFFRON sells pots and pans, herbs, spices, oils, soaps, and dyes from her spice kitchen stall.

BUZZ is a street vendor with all the gossip. He sells treats from a tray that's strapped around his neck.

KENZO the barber has a wig or hairpiece for every occasion, and is always happy to put his scissors to use!

COLONEL KARBUNCLE sells military uniforms, medals, flags, swords, helmets, cannon balls—all from the trunk of his old jeep.

PRU is a dreamer and Hannah's best friend. She likes to visit the market with Digby and Hannah, especially when makeup and dressing up is involved.

Mrs. BILGE pushes her dustcart around the market, picking up litter. Trouble is, she's always throwing away the objects on Mr. *Rummage's* stall.

Mr. CLUMPMUGGER has an amazing collection of ancient maps, dusty books, and old newspapers in his rare prints stall.

JAKE is Digby's friend. He's got a lively imagination and is always up to mischief.

CHRISSY's vintage clothing stall has all the costumes Digby and Hannah need to act out the characters in Mr. *Rummage's* stories.

PIXIE the market's fortuneteller sells incense, lotions and potions, candles, mandalas, and crystals inside her exotic stall.

YOUSSEF has traveled to many places around the world. He carries a bag full of souvenirs from his exciting journeys.